50

Michelle Kwan

SKATING LIKE THE WIND

LINDA SHAUGHNESSY

CRESTWOOD HOUSE
Parsippany, New Jersey

For Peter, Brian, and Keely Shaughnessy,
with Love

Acknowledgments

I thank the following people for helping me to make this book:

Shep Goldberg and Iana Dealey of Proper Marketing Associates for their enthusiasm and generous support.
Daniel Kwan, for his time, wit, and wisdom.
Cindy Lang of the Ice Castle International Training Center.
W.H. Long, for video support and those two perfect words.
Elise Feeley, reference librarian at Forbes Library.
Barb McCutcheon, who has been truly fun to talk to.
For sharing their photos: PMA, Barb McCutcheon, J. Barry Mittan, Lois Yuen, William Udell, and Sheila Foley.

For sharing their words: *American Skating World, The Hartford Courant, Skating* magazine, *International Figure Skating, Tracings, The Mobile Register, San Ramon Valley Times*, Barb McCutcheon, and the following sources for specific quotes.
Pages 32, 34, 37, 48: *Blades on Ice*, May/June 1995, "Michelle Kwan" by Marcia Burchstead and Dale Mitch and "1995 World Figure Skating Championships"; May/June, 1996, "Centennial on Ice."
Pages 14, 15, 24, 27, 32, 46: Reprinted courtesy of *The Boston Globe*.
Pages 50, 51: Reprinted courtesy of SPORTS ILLUSTRATED April 1, 1996. Copyright © 1996, Time Inc. "Red Hot" by E. M. Swift. All rights reserved.
Pages 25, 32, 33: Copyright 1995, USA TODAY. Reprinted with permission.
Pages 14, 16, 23, 37, 42, 46: *People Weekly*, 3/18/96, "At Rainbow's End" by Susan Reed et al. and 2/14/94, "In the Wings Waits Rising Star Michelle Kwan" by Michael Neill and Kurt Pitzer.

Elaine Streeter, Carol Weis, Nancy Carpenter, Tom McCabe, and the Hatfield writers and illustrators group.
Special thanks to my father and mother, William and Betty Lou Long; my outstanding mother-in-law, Eleanor Shaughnessy; and my family, Peter, Brian, and Keely.

Photo Credits

Front cover: Barb McCutcheon: t.r. Time, Inc./Sports Illustrated/Bill Eppridge: b.; Bill Frakes: t.l.

AP/Wide World Photos: 12. Barb McCutcheon: 39, 40, 43, 52, 53, 57. J. Barry Mittan: 4, 13, 17, 19, 22, 44. Proper Management Associates: 8, 25, 29, 31, 59. William Udell: 9. Lois Yuen: 34, 36, 37, 47, 48, 49, 55. Glossary Illustrations: © 1998 David Uhl Studios; Ice Backgrounds © 1998 Bruce Bennet Studios

Library of Congress Cataloging-in-Publishing Data

Shaughnessy, Linda.
    Michelle Kwan: skating like the wind/by Linda Shaughnessy.—1st ed.
    p. cm.—(Figure skaters)
    Includes bibliographical references (p.) and index.
    Summary: A biography of the American figure skater who, at the age of fifteen, won the 1996 World Championships.
    ISBN 0-382-39445-3. (lsb.)—ISBN 0-382-39446-1 (pbk.)
    1. Kwan, Michelle, 1980- —Juvenile literature.
2. Skaters—United States—Biography—Juvenile literature.
[1. Kwan, Michelle, 1980-. 2. Ice skaters. 3. Woman—Biography] I. Title. II. Series.
GV850.K93S53 1998
796.91'2'092-dc21
[B]   96-48350

Copyright ©1998 by Linda Shaughnessy

Cover and book design by Michelle Farinella

Published by Crestwood House
A Division of Simon & Schuster
299 Jefferson Road, Parsippany, NJ 07054

First Edition
Printed in the United States of America
10 9 8 7 6 5 4 3 2 1

CONTENTS

Michelle skates like a summer breeze to music from East of Eden at the gala at the 1996 World Championships.

1

BLADES AND ICE

She often says that skating is like being the wind...
• Lori Nichol, Michelle's choreographer

White light poured down on Michelle Kwan. It stuck with her as she moved alone over the ice to sad, sweet music. The eyes of 16,000 fans at the gala after the 1996 **World Championships** stuck with her, too.

She pushed across the ice with strong strokes. The **edges** of her blades caught hold and sent her flying, fast and free. She leaped and landed, swooping backward on one blade.

As steady as a wind-filled sail, she swept forward on one leg in a **spiral**, reaching back and up with her other leg. She froze into stillness, her costume fluttering in her breeze. Her face glowed with the flush of one who was doing what she truly loved.

Fifteen-year-old Michelle had power and grace, glitter and gold medals. Her love of skating began with the feeling of her blades against the ice. They could scrape, caress, or bite. They could slip or hold her weight on a sharp curve. Nothing else felt like blades on ice. The first time she tried skating, she knew she was going to be doing it for a long time.

Later she dreamed about where she might go on those blades—to the top of the skating world, to the Olympics. She set out on the quest.

She had many wise and loving people to guide her. A golden dragon medallion hung from her neck for luck. And Michelle had her own magic—the desire to try again and again, the knack for turning work into fun, and the powerful habit of believing in herself.

It was no wonder she was glowing as she coasted in that spotlight. She had taken a giant step closer to the end of her Olympic quest. The night before, in a contest that would stand out in the history of the sport, Michelle Kwan had become the ladies' figure skating champion of the world.

2

ONE DAY AT THE MALL

When I was younger, I was behind.
And then I caught up.
• Michelle Kwan, to *American Skating World*

On July 7, 1980, in the Chinese year of the monkey, Michelle Kwan was born in Torrance, California—a suburb of Los Angeles. Her father, Daniel, a native of Guangzhou (Canton), China, was a systems analyst, working with computers for a communications company. Her mother, Estella, had come to California from Hong Kong. She managed the family restaurant, the Golden Pheasant, in Torrance.

When Michelle was five, the Kwans lived near a shopping mall. At the mall there was an ice-skating rink. One day she and her sister, Karen, went to watch their nine-year-old brother, Ron, play hockey there.

Skating looked like fun. The girls asked their parents if they could do it, too. Karen, who was older by two years, was

It all began at the mall, in rented skates.

allowed to try it first. But a couple of weeks later, wearing a pair of rented skates, Michelle got her first sensation of blades on ice.

She held onto the boards around the edge for a while. "Like everyone else, I was slipping and falling at first," she remembered. But she loved every moment.

The girls began recreational skating lessons once a week in addition to swimming, piano, and gymnastics lessons. They got skates of their own, and in the summer of 1987 started actual figure-skating lessons. They learned how to stroke properly and glide and turn on the edges of their blades. Michelle wanted to do the **jumps**—the **toe loop, salchow, loop, flip, lutz,** and the more difficult **axel.** At first it took her longer than the other students to learn them, but she kept trying and soon caught up.

At her first skating competition, seven-year-old Michelle wasn't a bit nervous. All she had to do was skate her best, something she did every day. Competing with her friends felt like a game. She had fun, and she came in first, too.

Michelle was on the ice every week now, except once when she had the chicken pox. She was also in many more competitions, including one she remembers because of an embarrassing moment. When her name was announced, she stepped out onto the ice and immediately fell down!

When she and Karen competed against each other, sometimes Karen received higher scores than her sister and sometimes Michelle came out ahead. They always cheered each other on and encouraged each other in frustrating times. Danny and Estella had taught their children that family is important. These were the only brother and sisters they would have. They needed to be able to depend on each other.

In 1988, Michelle was watching TV as figure skater Brian Boitano won an Olympic gold medal for the United States. She liked the Olympic symbol of five rings she saw everywhere and all the flags waving. Boitano's flawless performance and high jumps inspired her. She decided that she would compete in the Olympics someday.

On roller skates in the garage, she and her friends acted out becoming world and Olympic champions. But behind the giggling, Michelle was serious. She knew where she wanted to go. If she couldn't get there today, tomorrow would have to do. But she would get there.

Michelle started her medal collection at an early age.

9

"LITTLE KWAN"

*If you skate, you have to have proper respect
for the sport . . . . You have to be honest from
your heart and dedicated all the time.*

• Danny Kwan, to the *San Ramon Valley Times*

As he watched his daughters skate, Danny Kwan noticed their natural ability. He also saw how hard they worked because they loved it so much. In spite of the expense of private lessons, as much as $90 each time for the two girls, he signed Michelle and Karen up with a world-class teacher, Frank Carroll. Carroll had coached champions Linda Fratianne and Christopher Bowman. A former school teacher, he was firm, kind, and even-tempered.

When Carroll saw Michelle skate, he saw something special in her. "You can look at someone the first time and tell if they have extraordinary talent or not, and she does have that," he told *Tracings* magazine. He also liked her attitude. At age 10, Michelle wanted to know what she had to do to succeed. When he told her, she set out to learn it right away.

As Frank Carroll's students, Michelle and Karen practiced movements they had already learned, improving their technique. They also worked on double and triple jumps, spinning two or three times around in the air before landing. Carroll felt that it was better for girls to learn these advanced jumps when they were young, before their bodies grew and matured.

In 1990 he became the skating director at the Ice Castle International Skating Center. It was in a town called Lake Arrowhead, nestled in the mountains about a hundred miles east of Los Angeles. The center had a private rink for training and a public rink open on three sides in nearby Blue Jay where skaters put on shows. It had equipment like harnesses for learning jumps. Skaters could use the weight room and spacious dance studio for off-ice training. They could relax tired muscles in the pool and jacuzzi. While skating, the students looked out on a panorama of pine trees.

The Ice Castle International Foundation offered scholarships to Michelle and Karen to spend weekends at Lake Arrowhead. On Fridays, Danny and the girls drove to the mountains. They had a lesson with their coach and hours of practice before returning home on Sunday night or Monday morning.

Michelle was on the ice with top-level skaters, some of whom she had seen on TV. She watched them and learned.

Michelle (left) and her sister, Karen, share some time on the ice.

Everyone there was focused on skating, pursuing their dreams.

Danny and Estella shared their daughters' dream. More and more of the family's time and money were invested in skating. There were bills for coaching, choreography, costumes, and skates. Travel to competitions was another expense. The Kwans made many hard decisions, one of which was to sell their house to pay for skating.

The next year the girls won scholarships to live at Ice Castle year-round. Eleven-year-old Michelle and 13-year-old Karen moved into one of many cabins at the training center. Danny stayed with them every night. After watching their morning practice, he drove 100 miles down the mountain to work. He returned every evening in time to tuck them in. Estella stayed in Torrance, managing the restaurant. She joined them in Lake Arrowhead on weekends if they didn't come home.

Michelle missed her friends from home. She wrote a lot of letters to them. But she had her best friend, her sister, with her, and before long all of the Kwans were part of the Ice Castle family. Michelle was called Little Kwan.

The beauty of the forest surrounding the training center amazed her. A squirrel came to visit her, and she built him a shelter and fed him. She loved animals, especially birds and her cat.

In her spare time Michelle went swimming or to a movie with friends. But most of the time she was training. Her parents told her that if she wanted to continue skating at this level, she had to pass up some of the fun things her friends at home were doing. Michelle didn't always like that, but she found fun in skating.

Considered a jumping marvel, Michelle could do all of the triple jumps except the triple axel, which was actually three and a half rotations. Only two women had ever done triple axels in competition—Midori Ito of Japan and Tonya Harding of the United States. Michelle was in awe of both of them.

Having advanced to the junior level, one step from the top, 11-year-old Michelle competed at the junior **Nationals** in January 1992. She expected to do well. But she had a bad day and ended up in ninth place.

Michelle warms up at the 1992 junior National Championships.

13

Instead of wallowing in disappointment, Michelle tried to figure out what she needed to change so that it wouldn't happen again. Frank Carroll looked ahead to the next year for a win at the junior level, and for the skating world to notice Michelle.

Michelle watched the 1992 Winter Olympics on TV. The 1994 Olympics beckoned, just two years away. She felt an urge to move closer to the action. "I wanted to be the youngest skater in seniors," she later told *The Boston Globe*. All she had to do to pass the senior test was to skate a freestyle program of jumps, **spins**, and **footwork** in front of a panel of judges. Michelle knew that she could do it.

Carroll wanted her to wait. He was away at a conference in Canada when the test was given in May. Michelle went against his wishes. "I knew I might get in trouble, but I just had to do it," Michelle later told *People* magazine. Her father took her to where the test was being given and she passed easily. Tiny 11-year-old Michelle Kwan was a senior skater.

4

THE BIG
LEAGUES

I was still a novice (at age 13). . . . I was doing double axels, triple toes, definitely not what she's doing. . . . it's incredible what she's accomplished.

• Kristi Yamaguchi, to *The Hartford Courant*

When Carroll returned, he was furious, but the deed could not be undone. "If I'm to be the captain of this ship, I will decide who's a mutineer and who is not," he told Michelle. "Now how do we go on?"

He explained the consequences of moving up to senior level. "You have to skate with polish and charm—it's not just about going out there and jumping your brains out." Michelle would have to train with more concentration. If she fell on a jump or missed an element while practicing a program, she had to keep going, as if it were a real performance.

She would be competing in front of thousands of people. There would be newspaper and TV reporters with cameras around, distracting her and wanting interviews.

Michelle seemed stunned. She had so much more to think about now. Her season as a senior skater would begin in December with regional and sectional competitions. If she did well, she could go to the biggest United States competition, the National Championships, in January. The top skaters from Nationals would go on to the World Championships in March.

Winning both sectionals and regionals, she showed that she was well qualified to skate in the 1993 Nationals in Phoenix. She was the youngest women's competitor at Nationals since Priscilla Hill in 1973.

When Michelle looked nervous, her coach and her father would tell her, "It's nothing, it's nothing." But one night Danny heard her moan those words in her sleep. He felt that he had been pushing Michelle too hard.

He had a talk with Michelle. "You are my daughter," he told her. "Skating has cost a lot of time and money and worry to your parents. But when I see you get too stressed out like this, I think it's time to quit."

But Michelle wasn't about to quit. It was fun to compete against "older" women. Nancy Kerrigan, then 23, was astonished to hear that she would be skating against a 12-year-old. At 12, Nancy had still been at the intermediate level.

With her black ponytail swinging, Michelle performed the required jumps, spins, and footwork of her technical, or **short program**. The next evening she did her freestyle, or

long program. She came in sixth place overall, two places behind Tonya Harding.

The United States Figure Skating Association (USFSA) decided to send Michelle to more competitions, starting with the Gardena Spring Trophy in Italy. They wanted international judges to see what she could do. Michelle enjoyed Italy, especially the food. And she won first place!

In July, shortly after her thirteenth birthday, Michelle competed in San Antonio, Texas, at the U.S. Olympic Festival, a mini-Olympics for up-and-coming United States athletes. At 4 feet 7 inches and 77 pounds, she was the smallest skater there.

She won the short program. The next night she skated her long program in front of 25,691 people, the largest audience ever at a figure-skating competition. Inspired by the crowd, Michelle gave a great performance. The Alamodome rocked with a standing ovation, and the judges gave her first-place scores again. Michelle had won!

In spite of all the attention she was getting, including being the cover story of October's *Skating* magazine, she felt like a regular kid. She liked to collect things, such as pins,

Wearing turquoise, her favorite color, Michelle reminds herself to stay cool and calm, take her time, and keep her landing leg under her at the Olympic Festival.

baseball caps, bottle tops, and trolls of all shapes and sizes. Trolls were good luck, she believed. She also had a golden pendant with a dragon on it, a gift of blessing from her grandmother when Michelle was born. She always wore it on a red cord around her neck.

Although Karen now attended the Rim of the World High School in Lake Arrowhead, Michelle picked up assignments once a week from middle school. She worked with a tutor so that she could have more time on the ice. The 1994 Olympics in Lillehammer, Norway, were only months away. Michelle knew it wasn't likely that she would be skating in them. But it wasn't impossible either.

She had two new programs for the coming season. With Frank Carroll and assistant coach Evelyn Kramer, Michelle worked on each element, improving her technique and increasing her speed. With Russian coach Irina Rodnina, she worked on footwork and flow. A new member of the Kwan team, Lori Nichol, choreographed the programs and helped Michelle show how the music felt. Lori's real mission was to awaken the artist in Michelle and free her to find her own expression.

Every autumn, top skaters competed in international events, fine-tuning their programs for their National and World Championships. The first event of 1993, Skate America, was in Dallas, Texas, and Michelle was invited.

She hoped to finish in the top five against competitors like world champion Oksana Baiul, French and European champion Surya Bonaly, and Tonya Harding of the United States. Most of the competitors had falls, and Harding's skate blade came loose. Michelle's solid skating earned her only seventh place, but more and more people became aware of who she was.

Although she was now at the senior level, Michelle was still eligible by age to compete at the World Junior Championships in Colorado Springs in late November. Her competitors included Irina Slutskaya, a bright and lively 15-year-old from Russia.

Michelle skated her short program without error. But in the long program, she turned a planned triple toe loop, the simplest triple, into a single. Her confidence began to leak away. Catching her coach's eye, she thought, "Okay,

Tiny Michelle makes a sizable impression at her first Skate America in 1993.

Frank, I'll do the next jump." She did the next five triples without a problem.

All that practice without stopping for mistakes was paying off. She won the long program and the overall competition. Michelle was the new world junior champion!

Of all her wins that year, this was the most important. She hoped it would show the judges at the upcoming Nationals that, even at 13 years old, she was one of the country's best skaters. Ordinarily those judges would also decide who would go to the Olympics in February.

But what happened was not ordinary at all.

5

DRAMA IN DETROIT

She always sees the positive in people . . .
when someone says something negative,
she in turn finds something positive.

• Lori Nichol, to *American Skating World*

The best skaters in the United States gathered in Detroit for the National Championships. The day before the start of the ladies competition, Michelle practiced alongside the favorites, Tonya Harding and Nancy Kerrigan, at Cobb Arena. Around 2:30 P.M., she followed Nancy off the ice and paused to pull her rubber guards onto her skate blades. Nancy, chatting with someone, walked behind the blue curtain that screened the passageway to the dressing rooms.

Suddenly a scream tore through the arena. Danny Kwan raced down from the stands, thinking it was Michelle. Frank Carroll had the same thought. Knowing it was Nancy, Michelle guessed that Nancy had tripped or had been hurt by a skate blade as someone was stretching. The truth was far

Michelle feels the ice and the music and tunes out everything else at the U.S. Nationals.

worse. A man had run up to Nancy, clubbed her over the knee with a hunk of metal, and bolted away, hurling himself through the glass arena door to escape.

Doctors who examined Nancy's leg determined that she would not be able to compete at Nationals. Security was tightened. Michelle and others worried about whether the attack had been specifically intended for Nancy or if any one of them could have been the target. The crowds of people had always seemed so friendly before. Would the attacker be caught? Would he strike again?

Trained to tune out distractions, Michelle skated well. When it was all over, Harding had won the gold medal, Michelle received the second-place silver, and the bronze medal went to Nicole Bobek.

The United States was allowed to send two women to the Olympics the next month. As silver medalist, Michelle was supposed to be one of them. It looked as if her dream had come true. Then it was announced that Nancy Kerrigan, if she recovered in time, would go instead. Michelle would be the first alternate.

"It's a bummer for me, but I was kind of hoping Nancy would be able to go. She deserves it," Michelle told *People* magazine without hesitation. Michelle understood that she herself would have more chances to go to the Olympics. She would be only 17 when the next ones took place in Nagano, Japan, in 1998.

She had to wait four more years for her dream.

6

HAVE SKATES,
WILL TRAVEL

*If I make it, I'll be happy. If I don't, I'll just
keep my head down and work hard.*
• Michelle, to *The Boston Globe*

The approaching Olympics and the attack on Nancy Kerrigan were hot news. Reporters and camera crews perched like vultures outside the Golden Pheasant, Michelle's family's restaurant. Some were permitted into the Ice Castle to talk to Michelle as long as they didn't interfere with her training.

She enjoyed meeting journalists and wisely said little about the attack. Even so, her father decided that he needed help handling the publicity and the many requests for her time. He asked agent Shep Goldberg of Proper Marketing Associates, who represented gymnast Mary Lou Retton, to become a member of the Kwan team.

Goldberg understood that there would be time later for Michelle to make money in shows and advertising. The most important thing now was to prepare for the Olympics. "This is a marathon, not a 100-yard dash . . . ," he told *USA Today.* "We've all agreed skating comes first, second, and third. Nothing should conflict with skating."

Soon after Nationals, police found out who had attacked Kerrigan. Three men were in on the plot to keep Nancy from competing, including Tonya Harding's bodyguard and her ex-husband. Suspicion fell on Tonya herself. As it seemed clearer that Nancy would recover and go to Lillehammer, it became less certain that Tonya would accompany her.

As first alternate, Michelle stayed prepared, skating her programs and doing weight training and ballet. She also did puzzles in the lodge and was silly with her sister and friends, as usual. She seemed to have no interest in the drama unfolding around her, except for the bottom line—who would compete in Lillehammer?

Many people thought that although she had little chance of winning a medal in Lillehammer, Michelle would be a more positive representative of the United States than Harding would be. Also, the experience would serve Michelle well in the future. But Harding's lawyers threatened to sue if

Michelle uses some unusual equipment for training in snowy places.

25

Tonya were taken off the team. In early February the USFSA decided to send Michelle somewhere near Lillehammer. If the situation changed at the last minute, she would be ready.

The Olympics began February 12, with Kerrigan and Harding in Lillehammer. Michelle, her father, and Frank Carroll arrived in Oslo, Norway, a few days later. On a rink all to herself, Michelle practiced in the mornings. The rest of the day, she shopped and attended Olympic events.

Michelle had fun, but she was not allowed to feel like a part of the U.S. team. She could not go into the Olympic Village. She had no team jacket or pin. The hardest part of all was to sit in her jeans and sweater, watching the ladies' competitions, yearning to be out on the ice.

In a press conference she focused on the positive things. She was honored to be there. She felt that things were probably working out just the way they should. It would make her work that much harder to be an Olympian in 1998.

Ukranian skater Oksana Baiul won the Olympic gold medal. Nancy won the silver medal, and Lu Chen of China received the bronze. After the Olympics, Kerrigan and Harding were scheduled to represent the United States at the World Championships in March. But Harding finally admitted to the criminal act of learning who had attacked Nancy and not telling the police. The USFSA banned her for life from skating in **amateur** competition. Nancy Kerrigan, exhausted by all that had happened, announced in early March that she would not skate at the World Championships either.

The alternates, Michelle and Nicole Bobek, traveled to Chiba, Japan. Michelle, who had been ready all along, finished fifth in her qualifying round. When Bobek didn't qualify, Michelle became the entire U.S. ladies' team.

Because of injuries, Olympic medalists Oksana Baiul and Lu Chen were also absent. Yuka Sato of Japan, Josee Chouinard of Canada, and Surya Bonaly of France were favored to win.

"I went to Worlds like I wasn't even there," Michelle told *The Boston Globe*. "I was just this molecule floating around. I was in awe of everybody."

She was excited to be competing against these top-level skaters. But in her short program, nervousness made her tentative. Performing without her usual spark, she finished in eleventh place. In her long program she went for everything, including seven triples. The judges placed her eighth in the long program, which boosted her up to eighth overall.

Thirteen-year-old Michelle was eighth among the best women skaters in the world! And her top ten finish allowed the United States to send two women instead of one to the next World Championships. She returned to Ice Castle, excited about the next season and happy because she had done her best.

7

GROWTH SPURT

It's how you move. It's not your age.
Artistry has nothing to do with age.
• Frank Carroll, to *The Hartford Courant*

Of all the things Michelle had missed in her travels, she was most happy to see her friends and relatives. She was glad that her next event, in April of 1994, was in Los Angeles in front of her hometown crowd.

It was a pro-am, a competition between **professional** and amateur skaters. Michelle's program had the greatest technical difficulty, but the exquisite artistry of professional Caryn Kadavy won first prize. Michelle came in second. Kadavy spoke about how nice Michelle was, how good she was for skating. "This is my time," Kadavy told *Skating* magazine. "But she is our future."

Michelle flew to Virginia that night to skate an exhibition performance the next day. Two days after that she arrived in Florida for the start of the Campbell's Soups Tour of World

Figure Skating Champions. Her mother went along to guide her through the challenges of life on the road and in the spotlight.

Michelle performed in cities across the United States with champions like Oksana Baiul, Elvis Stojko, and Brian Boitano, whose Olympic performance had inspired Michelle's dream. Watching them, she learned about skating and showmanship and makeup. Brian and Elvis helped with her triple axel. She squeezed in some homework, too.

When Michelle travels, her mother often goes with her.

In May, *Skating* magazine presented Michelle with their Readers Choice Award for 1993–94 Figure Skater of the Year. A month later the USFSA reclaimed Tonya Harding's gold medal from Nationals. But they didn't give it to Michelle. The Kwans were glad. Being handed a gold medal wouldn't make Michelle a champion. She had to earn that herself.

At almost 5 feet 2 inches and 96 pounds, Michelle had grown 7 inches and gained 19 pounds in two years. She looked stronger and moved with greater speed. But increases in weight and height change a skater's center of balance. Although she had good technique, Michelle still had to make adjustments.

She told *International Figure Skating*, "It's kind of different because you gain more muscles and stuff, and you have to use those muscles and put yourself in the air . . . ." She was having trouble with her triple loop but was confident that she would get over it.

The food served at Ice Castle was healthy. And Michelle was watchful of how much candy and soda she consumed, especially before competitions. She made a game out of creating nourishing treats such as chocolate milkshakes made with bananas, low-fat milk, sugar-free cocoa mix, and ice cubes.

Lori Nichol choreographed movements for new, more complex programs. Nothing would be changed as the season went on. If Michelle lost her focus, her muscles would "remember" what came next.

In August, Michelle came in second, behind Surya Bonaly, at the Goodwill Games in St. Petersburg, Russia. In October, on the outdoor rink at Sun Valley, Idaho, Michelle defeated the other top U.S. women skaters. In Pittsburgh at Skate America, she came in second to Bonaly again—a big improvement on her seventh—place finish the year before.

The next night she and Karen went trick or treating as Fred Flintstone and Pebbles. Few people recognized them, a relief for Michelle after so much exposure in the world spotlight. Her time with friends and family at Ice Castle was becoming rare and precious. Her mother now lived in the cabin with Michelle and Karen. Danny stayed in Torrance and joined them a few times a week. Her brother, Ron, was away at college.

In addition to her training, Michelle studied French, world history, English, algebra, and Chinese calligraphy with her tutor every afternoon. She did homework while eating lunch or at the lodge at night. The lodge had a big-screen TV for watching her favorite shows, including *Melrose Place* and *Beverly Hills, 90210*.

In November Michelle appeared on TV, along with champions Scott Hamilton, Katarina Witt, and others in *Disney's Greatest Hits on Ice*. She played Peter Pan with flying leaps and mischievous chases.

Around Christmastime, Michelle figured out what to do with the heaps of stuffed animals that fans had thrown onto the ice after her performances. They meant a lot to her, and she wanted to share the love they represented. She handed them out to patients at a children's hospital in Los Angeles, which she continues to do.

On the ice or off, Michelle follows her own advice: "Be yourself."

"After all, when you're sick, there's nothing like cuddling with your favorite bear or bunny," she told *Skating* magazine.

Because she had skated in top-level competitions that year, Michelle did not have to qualify for Nationals. But she was in the stands at sectionals and regionals, cheering for Karen. Chills of pride went through her when her sister won both and had her own moments of glory.

They were going to Nationals together! It was one more thing for the sisters, who were also best friends, to share.

8

GREAT EXPECTATIONS

I always talk about life with them.
I tell them that life isn't fair . . . You take
whatever you get and learn to be satisfied.
• Danny Kwan, to *USA TODAY*

The 1995 National Championships in Providence, Rhode Island, were the first since 1959 in which two sisters competed against each other. Karen, with her long arms and legs, had an ethereal, willowy style. She explained that while she envied Michelle's skating ability, she was not jealous of her sister. She told *The Boston Globe*, "We don't have any of that rivalry stuff."

Michelle agreed. "I'm skating for myself, and she's skating for herself. It's kind of fun and interesting," she told *Blades on Ice*.

Michelle had become a symbol of a bright future for United States figure skating. Most people expected her to become the new ladies' champion, the youngest one ever. Fans came through the snow and cold to watch her practices.

Shep Goldberg and Frank Carroll kept reporters away so that Michelle could focus.

Danny Kwan reminded his daughters that they were there to have fun. He told *USA Today*, "The bottom line is, what my wife and I expect from them is not a gold medal, but for them to have a happy life always."

Michelle's main competitors were 23-year-old Tonia Kwiatkowski from Ohio, who had earned a college degree while skating at the elite level, and 17-year-old Nicole Bobek. Although incredibly talented, Nicole had changed coaches frequently and was sometimes undisciplined about training. Nicole was a wild card. She could flop or win it all.

In Michelle's short program, skated to the *Yellow River* piano concerto, her footwork was crisp and accented the music nicely. But she rushed into the first part of her **combination jump.** Out of position, she couldn't do the second jump without taking steps in between. After a flash of dismay, she snapped back and focused on her next element.

The judges placed her third, with Tonia in first place and Nicole in second. Being anywhere in the top three allowed the possibility of winning, especially since the long program was worth twice as much as the short program.

The Kwan family spent the next day together, watching a movie and relaxing before going to the Civic Center for the evening's performances. Karen skated an excellent long

Michelle is known for the exquisite lines she makes with her body.

program, finishing in seventh place in the final standings.

Tonia skated, and then Nicole did her *Dr. Zhivago* program. She was brilliant, putting the pressure on Michelle, who was the last skater.

In a dress of cotton-candy pink, Michelle took the ice, determined to do a clean program to her classical music by Saint-Saëns. Her first jump, a double axel, was perfect. But as she was gliding across the ice for her second triple lutz, she realized that she didn't have enough speed. She rose in the air but couldn't get all the way around three times. She came down hard on her hip. Bouncing back up, she finished the program, but the damage was done.

She lingered on the ice, giving autographs and hugs. She didn't need to see her scores to know that the 1995 championship belonged to Bobek.

Michelle brought the silver medal home to Ice Castle and looked ahead to the World Championships in March. "You go from competition to competition, and if you do well or if you do badly, you never look back," she told *Blades on Ice.*

Surya Bonaly, who practiced **quadruple jumps** and landed **backflips** on one foot, would be the only skater at Worlds with as difficult a routine as Michelle's. Surya occasionally came to Ice Castle to work with Frank Carroll. Lu Chen of China also trained at Ice Castle at times. She had had a quiet year of recuperation from the foot injury that had kept her out of the 1994 Worlds and was skating well.

They all gathered in Birmingham, England. Michelle had a day off because those who finished in the top ten the year before didn't have to qualify. Instead of sitting around in the hotel getting nervous, she went to London to see Buckingham Palace and Big Ben, the famous clock in a tower of the Houses of Parliament.

On the first night of competition, she walked into the National Exhibition Center arena. Her hands were trembling. She had had trouble getting through this short program all season. But Surya Bonaly, who skated just before her, bungled a few jumps, which took some of the pressure off Michelle.

In a dress of swirly white and shades of blue, Michelle sprang into action and ticked off element after element. She was laughing at the end, her joy spilling over the crowd. When five judges gave her lower technical marks than they gave Bonaly, there was an outpouring of groans and boos. Michelle ended the night in fifth place.

Michelle couldn't keep from smiling as she neared the end of her long program.

The next evening she was again the last to skate her long program. The waiting was hard. Still the other women made enough mistakes so that if Michelle won the long program, the gold medal could be hers. The Kwan team, remembering her low marks in the short program, guessed that the judges wouldn't give Michelle the victory. But anything was possible.

It was a relief to step onto the ice and stroke to her starting position. People clapped along as she landed seven triples, including the one that had thrown her on her hip at Nationals. As she neared the end, she couldn't keep the smile from her face. She looked as if she wanted to skate forever.

The audience was on its feet before she finished, with the only standing ovation it had given all night. Overwhelmed,

Michelle covered her face with her hands, sobbing. Frank Carroll held back his own tears as they waited in the "kiss and cry" area for her scores.

The judges decided that it was the third-best long program. The gold, silver, and bronze medals went to Chen, Bonaly, and Bobek. Fourth-place Michelle was the only one who had skated both programs flawlessly, yet she was going home without a medal.

"There is nothing that I could have done better," Michelle told reporters. "I enjoyed my whole performance. I didn't really expect anything. . . . I just expected to skate well."

"The only thing I could think of was that she looked very young," said Carroll. "The judges were looking for the ladies' champion of the world, not the girls' champion of the world."

Three weeks later Michelle won a pro-am competition in Los Angeles, defeating both Bonaly and Bobek. It was the exclamation mark at the end of her season. It was a promise of things to come.

Danny and Estella Kwan watch Michelle's long program.

9

THE INSIDE
STORY

*What I like about Michelle is that what you see is
what you get . . . . Nothing with her is put on.*
• Frank Carroll, to *Skating* magazine

Through the spring and into summer of 1995, Michelle
delighted audiences as Peter Pan on the Tour of Champions.
On a two-day break, she met with Lori Nichol in Toronto to
work on programs for the next season. Lori played some music
she had been saving for the time when Michelle was ready.
Michelle fell in love with it.

In the past, Lori had shown Michelle what movements to
do to the music. This time Lori asked Michelle what she
would like to do.

Michelle skated around, showing Lori what she thought
others, like Brian Boitano or Oksana Baiul, would do.

Lori tried again. "Well, if someone was going to imitate
you," she asked Michelle, "what would they do?"

That made Michelle think. She started experimenting. At dinner they talked about being an artist and skating from the heart.

The music for her long program told the Biblical story of a girl named Salome (SA loh may), who danced for King Herod in return for the head of John the Baptist. At first Michelle was shocked at the idea of playing Salome on ice. Then she told *American Skating World,* "I think it's fun to tell a story and express how the characters would have felt . . . for the audiences to look at and use their imaginations."

Through the summer she worked with Frank Carroll on the technical aspects of her programs. She got stronger and faster. Her jumps were higher and covered more distance. Her goal was to have a triple/triple combination jump and maybe a triple axel in her new programs. She could do a triple axel but not consistently enough to put one into a performance.

Michelle played Peter Pan on the 1995 Tour of Champions.

As she skates, Michelle explores her feelings.

Carroll wanted to erase all doubt the judges might have about 15-year-old Michelle being mature enough to be a champion. He convinced her parents that she needed to wear makeup on the ice. "If you're appearing in the ballet, you have to look the part," he said. "We're not taking school exams, we're performing in front of thousands of people."

After asking family and friends for more ideas for her "new look," Michelle braided, clipped, and sewed her sleek black hair into a bun. Carroll insisted that she wear the bun all the time at competitions—no more ponytail. Judges watched practices, too, and good grooming would show them that she really wanted to do her best.

Late one night at the end of August, Michelle and Lori were making final adjustments to the programs. They were both tired. Michelle was skating without meaning, as if she had given up on the movements and was throwing them away. All that she had gained that summer seemed forgotten.

They stopped and talked. An artist has to respect each movement, Lori told Michelle. An artist has a story to tell. Once the music starts, she must be 100 percent committed, with her heart as well as her body.

Lori turned on the music again. Tears came to her eyes when she saw the change that had come over Michelle. ". . . It was like setting a bird free," Lori told *American Skating World*. Michelle was more than a skater. She was an artist.

10

THE WIND
RISES

To make money and maybe not reach your goal?
It's not a difficult decision for me at all.
• Michelle, to *People*

The 1995–96 season offered more opportunities for figure skaters than ever before. There were new shows, competitions, and tours, and there was a lot of money to be made.

Frank Carroll, Shep Goldberg, Danny Kwan, and Michelle planned out their season. They included events that would gain experience and exposure for Michelle. They turned down anything that would interfere with training, including a role in one of the *Nutcracker on Ice* casts that toured in December.

In August, in a bathing suit and sunglasses, Michelle skated on a rink set up on a California beach in the TV special *Too Hot to Skate*. In September she joined Elvis Stojko in his '95 Tour of Champions, a whirlwind trip from one coast of Canada to the other.

The full unveiling of the new Michelle came at Skate America in Detroit. As she warmed up with the other women for the short program, some spectators wondered who she was.

Her hair was pulled back tightly in a bun. Bright lipstick, eye shadow, eye liner, mascara, and blush highlighted her features. She looked captivating in her cranberry red costume.

Along with her new look, which pleased her, Michelle had a new resolve. She had been too nervous last year. This year she would go for everything. However, she had a little trouble with jumps in her short program to *Romanza*, Spanish flamenco music. The reigning world champion, Lu Chen, came in first, Irina Slutskaya was second, and Michelle was third.

The day of the long program was also Danny Kwan's birthday. Michelle dressed as Salome, in a deep purple harem costume with a flesh-colored middle. There were rhinestones

When spectators saw the mysterious-looking skater in the red dress, they wondered who she was.

43

Michelle turns into Salome.

and sparkles on her face and shoulders. As she began to move, she demanded attention, from her blades to the tips of her beguiling fingers.

For the first time in competition, she landed her triple/triple combination, though she was a little slow between the jumps. Near the end of the program, the music focused into a long, shrill note, as in a TV mystery when something is about to happen. Michelle's sweeping spiral added to the suspense. Then she launched into a double axel, skated a few quick steps, and was finished.

The audience showed their approval with a standing ovation and a cascade of stuffed animals and flowers. Relieved, Michelle became a 15-year-old again, shooting the air with her fingers like six-guns—bang—bang!

With first-place votes from six of the seven judges for her long program, Michelle moved into first place and won the gold medal. It was a marvelous birthday present for her father!

Skate America and four other international events had

been grouped into the Champions Series. Skaters could earn points in two of the competitions. The six skaters with the most points could compete in a final showdown in February. Competitors could receive prize money, too—up to $30,000 in each preliminary competition, $10,000 for making the finals, and $50,000 for winning there.

Michelle's competitions for points were Skate America and the Nations Cup, but she also skated in an extra one— Skate Canada, in New Brunswick. After watching the women warm up there, photojournalist Barb McCutcheon commented, "Despite the fact that the home favorite, Josee Chouinard, was on the ice, every eye was on Michelle. She definitely has incredible star quality."

Michelle's flamenco program won top scores this time. She missed the triple/triple combination in her long program, but the judges gave her the highest marks again. Michelle felt as if she were floating. She had won Skate Canada!

In late November in Germany, she won the Nations Cup, too, qualifying for the series finals with the highest number of points possible. She was interviewed on German television and then took off across the Atlantic and won a team pro-am in Philadelphia.

Finally she went home, bringing several additions to her gold medal collection. But it was not time to rest. The biggest events were yet to come.

11

OVERDUE REWARDS

*You are entering a time of great
promise and overdue rewards.*

• prediction from a fortune cookie
taped in Michelle's journal

"People who make predictions in skating are nuts," Frank Carroll told *The Boston Globe* before the 1996 Nationals in San Jose, California. "But Michelle has a good chance to be in the top three if she skates the way she has all year."

The current champion, Nicole Bobek, was competing with an injured ankle she had not rested, choosing instead to skate in a *Nutcracker on Ice* tour. Tonia Kwiatkowski, 1995 junior champion Sydne Vogel from Alaska, 13-year-old Tara Lipinski, and Karen Kwan were also in the running.

"I don't hope for gold medals," Michelle told *The Mobile Register*. "I just try to skate well and do the best I can. . . . You can always have a bad day and not win."

Skating early in the short program lineup, she landed

46

a textbook-perfect triple lutz/double toe loop combination. Her **layback** spins, **camel** spins, and sweeping spirals were enchanting. She finished in first place.

Tonia, with the highest marks from two of the judges, came in second. Nicole rose above her obvious pain to do a jazzy, crowd-pleasing performance for third place. Sydne Vogel was fourth and Tara Lipinski, with blindingly fast triple jumps, came in fifth. Karen, skating like a delicate ribbon floating on a breeze, was sixth.

Michelle laughs with Nicole Bobek at a press conference in San Jose.

The following evening, when Michelle emerged as Salome, she held nothing back. She nailed both jumps in her triple/triple combination and everything else until the end. During the long suspenseful note, her focus slipped. Instead of a double axel, she did a single one. Two seconds later when the music stopped, she stuck out her tongue, pointed a finger to her head, and fired, grinning.

Nicole then withdrew because of her ankle. Tonia's performance was elegant but not enough to top Michelle's, nor were any of the others' performances. Karen finished fifth

Michelle shares national glory with Tonia Kwiatkowski (left), Tara Lipinski, and Sydne Vogel (far right).

and Sydne was fourth. Tara Lipinski won the bronze medal, and Tonia took the silver. The gold medal went to Michelle Kwan, the new United States National champion.

In years past, skaters used the time between Nationals and Worlds to go home and train. This year Michelle did her training on the road. For a few weeks she skated in a mini-Tour of Champions.

After the mini-tour she traveled to St. Petersburg, Russia, for the celebration of the hundredth birthday of the World Championships. She fell ill with a cold and cough but chose to compete anyway and came in third.

"She's had a great year and you can't be wonderful all the time," Frank Carroll told *Blades on Ice.*

Four days later the Champions Series Finals began in Paris. Still not feeling well, Michelle landed in fourth place in the short program behind Lu Chen, Josee Chouinard, and the new European champion, Irina Slutskaya.

Irina's freestyle program was flawless. Lu Chen's was a disaster. Josee fell on a triple lutz. Then, alluring "Salome" danced over the ice, earning the highest marks of the night. Michelle vaulted from fourth place to first.

Having won four gold medals and $150,000 in all, Michelle was the queen of the Champions Series.

One question remained: Who would be queen of the world?

Michelle whirls through a busy season of competitions.

12

A CHANGE IN THE WIND

To have to be perfect, and then be
perfect, is a rare thing in skating.
• E.M. Swift, *Sports Illustrated*

Michelle arrived at the 1996 World Championships in Edmonton, Canada, with her teddy-bear backpack and her lucky pendant. She had been training at least six days a week, making her best even better.

In spite of her winning season, she thought of herself as the underdog next to reigning champion Lu Chen, Irina Slutskaya, and Midori Ito. Ito had returned to amateur skating after being professional for a few years.

In the days before the start of the ladies' competition, Michelle signed autographs and talked to kids. She painted and repainted her long fingernails with new colors and sparkles. Before she went to sleep at night, she ran through her programs in her head.

At last, it was time to skate.

After a season of refining her makeup, costuming, and movements, Michelle had blossomed. With a focused, mysterious air, she sprang into her flamenco program. From the exquisite sequence of spirals at the beginning to the coy look over her shoulder at the end, she was spectacular.

She felt as if she had just finished the best performance of her life. The 16,000 fans in the Northlands Coliseum resoundingly agreed. So did the judges, putting Michelle in first place, followed by Lu Chen and Irina Slutskaya.

Ever since she was a little girl, Michelle had dreamed of being a world champion. Now she was one performance away from making it a reality.

Irina was the first of the final six to skate her long program. She went sprawling on her opening triple lutz. Next Lu Chen skated her Rachmaninoff program with the delicacy of a butterfly. The Edmonton audience, realizing they had seen something extraordinary, chanted "six, six!" Few could remember the last time a woman skater had received a perfect score of six. The judges gave Lu Chen two of them.

Michelle and Frank Carroll were closeted in the little room for the girls who gather the flowers off the ice. Michelle heard the crowd roar for Lulu's performance and scores.

Panicked, she thought, "Oh God, I'll have to do a quadruple toe loop to win." Then she shook herself and said, "Just go

Michelle's program, including this layback spin, has to be almost perfect, and it is.

for it. Go for everything. Why not?"

Carroll knew that the bigger the challenge was, the better Michelle usually skated. He told her, "You've got to believe in yourself. You can do it."

Two more skaters performed, and then it was Michelle's turn. She scooped up some ice chips and let them melt on her hands and neck. She went over her strategy for the triple/triple combination jump. If she missed the second triple, then she would make up for it with a triple toe loop at the end of the program. Otherwise she would finish with a double axel—not a single one, as she had done at Nationals. She had to be perfect.

She became Salome, toying with the crowd as if King Herod himself were in the stands. When she got to the combination, she didn't do the second triple—it didn't feel right. Her excitement built as she maneuvered through her spins and leaps without error. Feeling about to burst through that long suspenseful note, she chopped it off with a grand triple toe loop. It was over!

She broke down, quaking with sobs. She saw the crowd on their feet, her father clapping with wide sweeps of his hands, her mother with both thumbs up. The chant "six, six, six!" rose again.

In the kiss and cry area, she cried out the tensions that she had bound up inside. "Don't be disappointed in how the results are," said Frank Carroll. "You skated fabulously!"

"Yeah," she answered. "I feel that too."

When the scores were posted, people gasped. They were witnessing figure-skating history. Michelle had two perfect sixes also!

After the last skater performed, the results were official. Irina Slutskaya had won the bronze medal. Two women had skated programs worthy of the gold medal. But Michelle's scores were slightly higher than Lu Chen's. Fifteen-year-old Michelle Kwan was the new world champion!

Michelle holds the gold.

13

Around the Bend

...Whatever you do, have fun. ... Life is very short and I think you have to go out and enjoy it.

• Michelle, to *American Skating World*

After performing Sunday in the gala that ended the World Championships, Michelle left Edmonton on an overnight flight. She still found it hard to realize that she had won.

There was little time to think about it. On Monday and Tuesday she led her team to victory at the Hershey's Kisses Challenge in Boston. She was interviewed in New York on Thursday by David Letterman on his TV show. On Friday she flew to Florida to start the Tour of Champions.

And so her life would go on, as she continued her quest for a chance to skate at the Olympics. As a spokesperson for the Children's Miracle Network, she had many public appearances to make. In June she was named a spokesperson for Campbell's Soups in her first agreement to advertise a product.

Performing as Pocahontas in the 1996 Tour of Champions, Michelle thinks of her home at Lake Arrowhead.

On National Girls and Women in Sports Day, Michelle answered questions about her career in an online computer chat. She was honored at the White House, named Skater of the Year a second time, and was a finalist for the prestigious Sullivan Award, given for character, leadership, athletic ability, and being an admirable amateur athlete. Sixty of the greatest skaters of all time left handprints and initials in the new USFSA Walk of Fame in Colorado Springs, Colorado. Michelle was one of them.

Some people have questioned whether the lifestyle Michelle experienced was healthy for a child. "What have I missed?" she asked *The Mobile Register*. "I meet new people. I travel. There are so many extras I've had in my life because of skating."

One of those extras is relief from financial worries. In the 1995–96 season, Michelle reportedly earned over $800,000 from skating. She bought a jeep to travel the mountain roads around Lake Arrowhead, although what she really wanted was a slick Italian sportscar.

She said that taking the road test for her driver's license when she turned 16 was scarier than skating at the World Championships. She was so nervous that she botched her three-point turn and flunked! But she passed on her second try.

As lucrative as skating had become for Michelle, the Kwans believed that a good education offered better options for the future. While continuing to compete and perform, Karen started college in the fall of 1996. At her high school in Lake Arrowhead, Michelle did science labs and took French tests. When she was away from home, she turned in her assignments by E-mail on her laptop computer. She wanted to go to Harvard and perhaps become an attorney, when her Olympic quest was over.

Frank Carroll would make no predictions about Michelle's staying on top over the next few years. There were many excellent skaters, and others with great promise coming along. Being the world champion, the one everyone was trying to beat, was especially hard. In the 1996-97 season Michelle continued her winning streak, despite problems with ill-fitting skates and a sore ankle. And then, having a bad day, she skated a disastrous long program at the 1997 Nationals. Tara Lipinski slipped by her into first place, stunning everyone.

But when things get tough, champions get tougher, and Michelle is a champion. She learns more every day, about skating and about herself, as she works on new jump combinations,

Michelle and coach Frank Carroll are a team working toward their Olympic goal.

on her triple axel, and on exploring the artist within her. On her own, she choreographed a new program, "Winter," to a Tory Amos song. She dedicated it to a friend, Tour of Champions director Harris Collins, who passed away suddenly in June of 1996.

Michelle's training in the sport she loves has also been training for life. "I love competition, striving to skate my best, the pressure to do it right, right now," she told *The Mobile Register.*

"I also love working hard. It disciplines me and helps me get my priorities straight. And I love performing for an audience. It's like being an actress or a ballerina."

Skating has been fun, and fun is something Michelle will probably take with her on every quest.

"Right now, it's a perfect life," she said. "This is all my dream, and it's really come true."